# SOUTH AFRICA
## the world in one country

SUNBIRD
PUBLISHING

First published 2001
2 4 6 8 10 9 7 5 3 1
Sunbird Publishing (Pty) Ltd
34 Sunset Avenue, Llandudno, Cape Town, South Africa
Registration number: 4850177827

Publisher Dick Wilkins
Editor Brenda Brickman
Designer Mandy McKay
Production Manager Andrew de Kock

Reproduction by Unifoto (Pty) Ltd, Cape Town
Printed and bound by Tien Wah Press (Pte) Ltd, Singapore

ISBN 0 62403 973 0

DEDICATION
For Grant and Ilse, and our Little One – welcome to a brave new world.

PREVIOUS PAGE *Yzerfontein on the Cape West Coast has a stark, almost surreal beauty.*
BELOW *The tiny flightless dung beetle shares a home with the giant mammals of the Eastern Cape's Addo Elephant National Park.*
RIGHT *Lifeless only in appearance, at least one specimen of baobab in the Kruger National Park is known to be over 1 000 years old.*
OVERLEAF *A series of jagged, needle-like peaks makes up the rocky slopes of the Karoo's Valley of Desolation.*

# CONTENTS

# SOUTH AFRICA – THE WORLD IN ONE COUNTRY

**ABOVE** *Via the cableway, visitors make their way up the landmark that is Table Mountain to marvel at the city below and the ocean beyond.*

Nowhere across the entire length and breadth of this remarkable continent that is Africa is there a place so varied in its landscape, so diverse in its cultural heritage and so distinct in its temperament as South Africa. From mountain to sea, desert to savanna, every tree, shrub, bird and reptile differs from one to the next. Juxtaposed against the unforgiving backdrop of desert dunes are the delicate blooms of spring-flowering mesembs, against the deep blue skies the powerful wings of a raptor, and against the orange-burnt sunset the silhouette of traditional mud-and-daub huts. And yet, despite all these variations in colour, shape, texture and mood, there is an extraordinary affinity with the spirit of the land, a disposition that embraces the unity of it all.

From the remotest of places almost forgotten by time and the mysteries of age-old customs to the cityscape of a great metropolis and the flurry of contemporary urban culture, the people and places of South Africa offer a fascinating look at the ever-changing face of a great continent and its long-cherished legacy of diversity.

From the fynbos-bedecked slopes of Table Mountain to the blistering heat of the Lowveld, the South African horizon is punctuated with acacia and mopane woodland, rural settlements and rolling beach dunes, broken by the outline of an occasional baobab, or the rocky ridge of the Great Escarpment. This unparalleled diversity of landscape and colour is what makes South Africa unique, and what has prompted the remarkable interest it enjoys from people across the globe.

For intrepid travellers and adventurers, the prime attraction is the country's unrivalled wildlife heritage, at its most impressive in the big-game regions of Mpumalanga, KwaZulu-Natal and the Eastern Cape. In terms of species diversity, South Africa ranks third in the world, behind the wild places of Indonesia and the rainforests of the Amazon Basin. As a result, there are no less than 17 national parks, and more than 500 smaller reserves, protected by law to conserve not only the wildlife and unique plant life, but to preserve the distinctive scenic character of the subcontinent. While some conservationists argue that conservation fundamentally means the restoration of the environment to its original state, others maintain that conservation should be 'for the people' and that the eternal conflict between humankind and the world in which we live can only be resolved by compromise. If both man and nature are to survive the apparent clash of ideals prevalent in the First World, the realm of wild animals – and the plants and trees that support them – must also be the domain of human conscience, in which the ultimate goal is mutual benefit and a shared responsibility. Much the same is true, of course, between the various cultures that people South Africa, from the Xhosa to the Zulu, the Venda to the Sotho. All too often in communities across the global village, one tradition is sacrificed for another, one custom discarded for another, all under the mantles of 'progress' and 'development'. However, although these dangers certainly do persist in a region that is rapidly embracing the attractions of a First-World society, South Africans have, in the most part, adopted a remarkable sense of tolerance, at least when it comes to social and cultural differences. And it is this spirit of mutual respect and acceptance that will make it the model for the rest of a continent that is all too frequently plagued by conflict and dissension.

Of all the different faces that merge here in the subcontinent to form the unmistakable image of South Africa, the most recognisable must be that of Table Mountain, Cape Town's most enduring landmark. Originally populated only by the San hunter-gatherers that walked its pristine beaches, today the Mother City and the vast expanses that comprise its perimeters are peopled by an eclectic mix of cultures and communities, some traditional in their outlook, others entirely cosmopolitan in lifestyle.

Xhosa-, English- and Afrikaans-speaking businessmen work from the imposing office towers that run the length of the streets that lace the city

ABOVE *A caravan of camels transforms the white sands of False Bay's popular Long beach into a scene from* Laurence of Arabia.

ABOVE *Despite its ancient origins, hand-spinning remains a thriving cottage industry in Knysna.*

ABOVE *Although autumn sees the Hex River Valley take on hues of gold, in summer it becomes the 'valley of abundance'.*

ABOVE *A community of African, or jackass penguins at Boulders Beach are the most recent settlers to colonise the Cape.*

ABOVE *In contrast to the safaris that draw adventurers to Africa, the ski resort at Tiffendell offers a winter playground.*

ABOVE *The African elephant, largest of all land mammals, has come to symbolise the indefatigable spirit of the African bushveld.*

ABOVE *The coelacanth was thought to be extinct until a living specimen of the 300-million-year-old species was rediscovered in 1938.*

ABOVE *South Africa's culinary tradition is extremely varied, and greatly influenced by the spices introduced by slaves from the East.*

centre; civil servants and spiritual leaders serve the citizens and congregations that make up the people of Cape Town, from the urban communities of the Bo-Kaap on the edge of the city to those of the semirural suburb of Hout Bay.

Beyond the city limits, the famed vineyards of the winelands to the north make way for the semiarid veld of the Overberg and Little Karoo, and the temperate climes of the West Coast stretch into the flowering fields of Namaqualand. This is an entirely different face of the Cape. Rural communities here ply the land, tilling the soil and harvesting fruit; some fish the oceans, while others depend on the sale of crafts created in the tradition of their forefathers. The world in which these people live is a simple one, acted out against a backdrop of some of the country's most spectacular scenery – from the nutrient-rich orchards of the Boland and the rugged outcrops of the Cederberg to the wooded slopes of the Outeniqua range and the coastal paradises of Knysna, Plettenberg Bay and Nature's Valley along the scenic Garden Route.

Whereas much of the Western Cape is covered by gentle plains, wooded hills and tranquil vistas, the Northern Cape, on the other hand, is a land in contrast. In parts arid and desolate, the parched wilderness of the northwestern regions, incorporating the vast expanse of the inhospitable Great Karoo, borders the wide open spaces of Namibia and Botswana. Skirting the skyline here are the settlements of the descendants of semi-nomadic Khoisan, who have set up home amid the stands of thornbush and aloe, while herds of springbok and gemsbok tread the dry riverbeds. The wonder of nature is at its most exceptional here – small emerald-green shrubs emerge from a desiccated soil that may not have seen a drop of rain for years; the dry air is suffocating, and yet gives breath to a remarkable array of life; on occasion, raging waterfalls plummet from rocky plateaux; and, at the most brilliant of sunsets, the blistering heat of day gives way to icy cold night. Here too are the succulent grasses that nurture the flocks of sheep essential to the local economy, and the hardened dolerite that make up its soils yields the world's most famous diamond deposits, which in turn sustains a national economy.

The landscape of the Eastern Cape, which skirts the country's eastern coastline between the Western Cape and KwaZulu-Natal, provides a very

ABOVE *Dotted with* umuzi *(homesteads), the undulating hills of KwaZulu-Natal are the traditional home of the Zulu nation.*

different portfolio of images. Blessed with plenty of wildlife, wide beaches and green hills, the Eastern Cape is not only the traditional home of the Xhosa-speaking Nguni people, who crossed the Great Kei River to settle here long before the white man set foot on these shores, but also a seat of European power during the colonial era. Both the Xhosa and the descendants of the white settlers who established colonies here in the 1800s call this land of extraordinary beauty home. Today, although the Eastern Cape retains many of the more enduring features of its colonial past – fine examples of Victorian architecture and a widely acclaimed tradition in academia – it is its exceptional natural heritage that takes pride of place on its list of success stories. The Wild Coast is an evergreen wilderness of lazy lagoons, sandy coves and abundant rivers surrounded by thick woods, rolling hills and stony cliffs. These, in turn, are home to the herds of mountain zebra and elephant that have been established in the region's protected parklands. With all this natural splendour, it is little wonder then that this rugged stretch of land is a naturalist's haven: the craggy peaks of the Witteberg, a string of private game lodges, an untamed ocean ideal for surfing, and even the indulgence of the impressive ski resort at Tiffendell.

But if the majestic Eastern Cape is an adventurer's dream, then KwaZulu-Natal is every inch its competitor. Steeped in a rich and often volatile history played out on the battlefields of the Anglo-Boer War, the Anglo-Zulu wars and smaller intercultural skirmishes, this Garden Province has, in many respects, shed the oppressive mantle of its troubled past to become an adventurer's playground and a kingpin in the nation's

all-important leisure industry, boasting exceptional fishing grounds, choice golf courses and some of the best surfing waters anywhere in the country. From the scenic wonder of the Drakensberg range that forms part of the Great Escarpment to the breathtaking beauty of its sparkling beaches and a series of some of the country's finest national parks and game reserves,

ABOVE *The Drakensberg's foothills harbour small pockets of tranquillity, such as Kenmo Lake near Himeville.*

ABOVE *Large tracts of the Free State have been successfully cultivated, entrenching it as the heartland of the country's agricultural industry.*

ABOVE *Like the Sotho, many of South Africa's indigenous people have retained much of their tradition – even in the face of Western influence.*

KwaZulu-Natal – home of the world-famous Comrades marathon between Durban and Pietermaritzburg – is a diverse region of wide open spaces comprising vast expanses of unspoilt coastline and estuarine wilderness to immense urban settlements, most notably Pietermaritzburg, Howick and the country's most vital port Durban, which highlight the province's great cityscape. The earliest inhabitants who trod this pristine landscape were the San, who chronicled the story of their extraordinary heritage in the numerous rock paintings that adorn the walls of caves and rockfaces. Today, however, the people of KwaZulu-Natal are a varied group made up of the proud Zulu nation, the Indian communities originally brought in to work the extensive fields of sugar cane, and the South Africans, who trace their ancestry back to the British settlers of the early 1800s.

Beyond the physical wall created by the natural barrier that is the Great Escarpment lies a very different panorama of wild cosmos and golden sunflowers basking under a dazzling sun, cultivated fields of maize and

wheat waving in the wind, productive sheep and cattle farms, weathered rock formations carved by wind and sand, and great plains yielding diamonds and gold, platinum and coal. This starkly beautiful landscape of the Free State – epitomised by the majesty of the eastern highlands – is host, too, to populations of Tswana and Sotho, many of whom still lead largely rural lifestyles.

Like so many of the traditional cultures that permeate the heart of South Africa, some individuals and groups have chosen to remain faithful to age-old customs and beliefs, following the ways of their forefathers. There are those, on the other hand, who have embraced contemporary society, settling in urban enclaves, adopting Western dress and participating fully in the socio-economic and political structures of the latter-day South Africa. In fact, although ancient cultures and customs continue to play a pivotal role in the daily lives of many black South Africans, the modern trappings of Western life still have significant influence on the lifestyles of

ABOVE *In a world of microchips, some rural parts of South Africa still offer a rare opportunity to experience the steam power of a bygone era.*

ABOVE *The Pondo dancers at Shakaland, Eshowe, keep their heritage of traditional music and rhythmic dance alive in a modern society.*

ABOVE *Even in plush Johannesburg suburbs such as Bryanston, curio-sellers market traditional crafts mastered by their ancestors.*

ABOVE *Johannesburg is built on ground originally cleared for traditional homesteads and later the canvas tents of the gold rush.*

South Africa's indigenous people. With the exception of a few small pockets of truly authentic cultural practices, most traditional communities have adopted at least some elements of modern society, and to safeguard the enormously rich cultural heritage of black South Africa, dotted throughout the country are preserves that serve as reminders of the way of the ancestors. While KwaZulu-Natal has the impressive Shakaland cultural village honouring the Zulu tradition, the Eastern Cape has Kaya Lendaba, in honour of the Xhosa-speaking groups; Tsonga Kraal is dedicated to the Tsonga-Shangaan people of the Northern Province, and the Free State boasts Botshabelo cultural village, the traditional 'place of shelter' of the Pedi, South Ndebele and other groups who found refuge here.

To the north and northwest, in what are simply known as South Africa's Northern and North West provinces, are the equally fascinating traditional homelands of colourful indigenous peoples, among them the Venda, Sotho, Tswana, Ndebele, Mfengu and Barolong, and similar small communities who have lived on these rough and, in places, rather austere plains for centuries, leaving behind such fascinating reminders of their contribution to the nation's cultural heritage as the awe-inspiring ruins at Mapungubwe, one of South Africa's richest and most impressive archaeological and historical sites. This is the land of the Soutpansberg, Magaliesberg and Pilanesberg, each dotted with settlements established by early indigenous groups fleeing the terror of Zulu king Shaka's expansionist military

ABOVE *Even today, the family unit remains the nucleus of traditional communities of the Ndebele and other indigenous peoples.*

ABOVE *Forerunners in the liberation struggle, Mandela and Mbeki have emerged as champions of South Africa's unified face of democracy.*

ABOVE *Flag-waving supporters cheer Bafana Bafana, South Africa's national soccer team.*

ABOVE *In an industry that relies on foreign visitors, domestic travel to hotspots such as Kruger has proved vital to the country's tourist market.*

campaign and the battlegrounds that played witness to the bloodshed of the Anglo-Boer War between the British colonialists and Boer commandoes. Thankfully, the battlefields of old have given way to expanses of wildlife sanctuary – prime among them Madikwe Game Reserve – and other havens that protect the region's natural history, including isolated groves of lonely cycads and baobabs and an endless parade of birds and other wildlife. Rising amid the craggy outcrops on these arid plains is the vision of the fantastical Sun City and the magnificent Palace of the Lost City, a twentieth-century wonderland of lively casinos and sprawling entertainment venues, originating more in the fantastical imagination of their creators than in authentic African mythology. The contrast of soaring turrets and gold-inlaid minarets in a lush landscape of waving palms and dense forest set against a backdrop of a dry and dusty Highveld, Africa's kingdom of pleasure offers an exciting illusion of a long-forgotten world. Here, deep in an Africa best illustrated by the pens of esteemed fantasy writers such as Rudyard Kipling and Rider Haggard, are elegant interiors of marbled floors and crystal chandeliers, where exquisitely carved columns support gilded domes reaching high into the African sky.

Just a few hours' drive away, are the equally unforgettable but infinitely more real skylines of Johannesburg – South Africa's greatest metropolis – and its sister city Pretoria. A steady drone of traffic permeates the neon-lit modern highrises and Victorian facades, which line the highways and wide old streets. In Johannesburg, huge mine dumps loom high above the suburbs that rose from the small tented communities who settled here during the heyday of the gold rush in the 1800s, while the thoroughfares of stately old Pretoria, for years the seat of the country's administrative powers, are festooned with lilac-flowered jacaranda trees. Along with the adjoining 'townships', or rather satellite cities of Soweto and Alexandra, these dusty streets yielded national icons Mandela and Mbeki, and others who continued the struggle for universal suffrage against overwhelming odds.

ABOVE *The Easter gathering of the Zionist Church draws some two million worshippers.*

ABOVE *With all its diversity, it is the scenic splendour of regions such as the Blyde River Canyon that remains South Africa's most significant treasure.*

Lively shebeens and thundering techno-pop raves form but a small part of an exhilarating nightlife that spills over into the streets – and into the early hours of the morning. This is also a world where the grandeur of nightspots such as the spectacular Caesar's Palace and the charm of Gold Reef City are second only to the elegant glass-fronted malls of Hyde Park and Sandton Square. The excitement of these vibrant settings are even further enhanced not only by the attractions that draw visitors to the Randburg Waterfront and the festivities of the annual Rand Show, but also travellers and locals enchanted by the rhythmic beat of the mine dancers and the hoards of fans who flock to the sport stadiums to cheer on their soccer heroes. Apart from the popular drawcards that attract visitors to the city centres, there are also a number of more leisurely pastimes with which the province of Gauteng has become synonymous: hiking through the nature reserves, and sailing, fishing and waterskiing on the dams that punctuate the city limits.

Again, just hours from the two bustling cities of Johannesburg and Pretoria, is the scenic wonder of Mpumalanga, with its waterfalls, country lodges, plantations of forest and orchards. The site of fascinating archaeological ruins – most significant among these the ruins at Thulamela – and boasting South Africa's greatest variety of flora and fauna, these northern stretches of the country are a natural paradise that includes within its boundaries the finest national park and private game reserves the continent has to offer. The wildlife here is its primary resource, and finds its pinnacle in the world-famous Kruger National Park. Covering more than 20 000 square kilometres (7 720 square miles) between the Crocodile and Limpopo rivers, Kruger – like many of the area's private reserves – boasts an enormous diversity of wildlife, top among them lion, leopard, rhino, elephant and buffalo, which comprise the Big Five, and some 500 different species of birds. Equally impressive is the region's wide variety of indigenous vegetation, which provides an ideal habitat for a similarly unique array of birds and animals. Kruger – the jewel in Africa's conservation crown – takes visitors through some of the most spectacular scenery in Africa and offers a first-hand look at what the nation may lose should its natural heritage be neglected. But there is so much more to South Africa than the wonder of its wildlife, the diversity of its extraordinary landscape and the rich cultural heritage of its many people – these are the contrasting faces of South Africa, and the legacy it has to offer. Off the beaten track, isolated from the quaint villages, towering cityscapes and well-trodden hiking paths are endless vistas of South Africa, the world in one country.

# WESTERN CAPE

*Lashed by the pounding waves of the Atlantic and long hailed as the Cape of Storms, the Cape Peninsula and its immediate interior is, in reality, a very different world of gentle mountain slopes, fynbos and forest and verdant vineyards, its people a happy mix of cultures that lends the Western Cape its unique character.*

From the craggy seascape of rocks and untamed beach that form Cape Point to the flat summit of Table Mountain and beyond into the fertile vineyards of the interior, the Western Cape is, above all, a land of contrasts. As the country's most significant tourism drawcard, Cape Town boasts a vast array of attractions that continue to draw throngs of sightseers to its pristine peninsula. Looming above the modern city centre, alive with a frenetic activity that rivals many of the world's most industrious First World capitals, are the edifices of Signal Hill, Devil's Peak and the rounded buttress of Lion's Head. But prime among these instantly recognisable peaks is the stony face of Table Mountain.

At the foot of the magnificent mountain, skirting the shores of Table Bay, lies Cape Town's most ambitious and, indeed, successful development project, the Victoria & Alfred Waterfront. Built on land originally reclaimed from the sea in the first half of the twentieth century, and incorporating the docks that continue to serve this important port city, the Waterfront development comprises the Victoria Wharf – one of the city's most impressive shopping malls, a series of plush hotels, the acclaimed Two Oceans Aquarium and a seemingly endless sea of restaurants and entertainment venues. Beyond, just kilometres from the bustling seafront, lies Robben Island, isolated from the mainland by the tumultuous ocean, and today acknowledged throughout the world as the spiritual home of South Africa's long struggle for democracy.

The Western Cape extends, however, far beyond the confines of the Mother City, its sandy beaches stretching up both the rugged West Coast and along the southeastern seaboard that comprises the spectacular Garden Route. Inland lie the modern entertainment complexes of the city's Northern Suburbs, the spring-flowering veld of Namaqualand, the untamed wilderness of the Cederberg and, beyond, the charming hamlets and rural settlements of the Boland, the Overberg and the Little Karoo.

RIGHT *Cape Town, with its ever-popular Victoria & Alfred Waterfront and instantly recognisable Table Mountain, is South Africa's undisputed leisure capital.*

TOP *Plagued by a painful history, Robben Island – off the coast of Table Bay – has emerged as one of the country's few World Natural Heritage Sites.*
ABOVE *At the very tip of the rugged peninsula lies the expanse of inviolate beaches and rocky mountainscape that comprise Cape Point.*
RIGHT *Virtually surrounded by craggy mountain and natural splendour, Cape Town's City Bowl is a hubbub of cosmopolitan society.*

TOP  In contrast to the economic, political and social responsibilities faced by the First World metropol at the foot of Table Mountain, the Mother City has also emerged as one of the continent's top leisure resorts, attracting kite-surfing enthusiasts and other adventurers to its pristine beaches.

ABOVE  Notwithstanding the metropolitan feel of the great urban centre, Cape Town's awesome expanse of wave-ravaged ocean has earned it an enviable reputation as one of the world's surfing hotspots.

RIGHT  Cape Town's sun-kissed beaches, such as those of Clifton on the Atlantic Seaboard, have been acclaimed as Africa's finest stretches of unspoilt coastline.

TOP  *The rich cultural heritage of latter-day Cape society focuses largely on the coloured community, proud descendants of the European colonists and Eastern slaves who settled here from the mid-1600s.*
ABOVE AND RIGHT  *An age-old tradition in celebration of the Prophet's birthday is the Islamic custom of Riempies Sny, where Muslim girls cut strips (riempies) of leaves, lay them in fragant oil and pack them into paper or fabric pockets to make sweet-smelling sachets, which they distribute among the community.*

OPPOSITE TOP *Established in 1913, Kirstenbosch National Botanical Gardens – recognised the world over as one of the finest floral reserves on the continent – are a haven of indigenous fynbos and natural forest, which includes approximately 7 000 species of indigenous plants, many of which occur naturally within the confines of the sanctuary.*

OPPOSITE BOTTOM *The gardens of Kirstenbosch lay sprawled across some 500 hectares (1 234 acres) of the eastern slopes of Table Mountain. Together the gardens and mountain form a vital element of the recently established Cape Peninsula National Park, which covers the entire peninsula and parts of its coastal waters.*

BELOW *Although Kirstenbosch lays claim as one of the Mother City's most prominent tourism drawcards, it is also an internationally acclaimed research station, with more than 35 hectares (86 acres) given over exclusively to cultivation and science.*

RIGHT *As a natural haven of largely endemic plant species, Kirstenbosch also occasionally acts as a showcase for local art and indigenous crafts from both South Africa and its neighbours, including Zimbabwe, where these stone sculptures were carved.*

LEFT  Many of the Mother City's attractions take advantage of its proximity to the mighty Atlantic. Not the least of these drawcards is the city's great sailing tradition, the nucleus of which are the marinas of the Royal Cape Yacht Club.

TOP  The two million litres of seawater that fill the enormous glass tanks of the Two Oceans Aquarium are home to marine life – predators to kelp forests – from both the Atlantic and Indian oceans.

ABOVE  Century City's grand new Canal Walk shopping complex was built in opulent style along waterways lined with 'a hundred shops and a thousand things to do'.

OPPOSITE  Prime among the developments on the city's seafront is the Victoria & Alfred Waterfront, with gracious new hotels such as the lavish Table Bay and boat moorings dotted along the water's edge.

THESE PAGES *The more than 27 000 hectares (66 000 acres) that cover the West Coast National Park comprise a coastal paradise, varying from bizarre rock formations such as those of Vingerklip (top) to wild expanses of flower-bedecked veld such as those at the Postberg Nature Reserve (above). Also punctuating this rough and hardy landscape are desolate beaches, languid lagoons and stretches of tidal marshland (right).*

TOP  *The fertile Cape interior is a gentle land cultivated with the vineyards and orchards for which historic Boland towns such as Tulbagh are famed.*

ABOVE  *The rocky slopes of the Simonsberg form a startling contrast to the fertile vineyards that cover the valley floor.*

RIGHT  *Although the heart of the winelands lies inland of Cape Town, much of the vine stock that helped establish these fine estates originates from the stock  planted on the peninsula's first vineyards, such as those of Groot Constantia.*

**TOP AND ABOVE** *The high rainfall of the Cederberg Wilderness Area (top) facilitates not only a prolific floral variety – as showcased in the Clanwilliam Wild Flower Garden (above) – but also feeds the Olifants River that supplies water to the region's fruit orchards, wheat fields and vineyards.*

**RIGHT** *Dwarfed by the magnificence of the great Cederberg range, the district of Clanwilliam shares its mountainous landscape with the famed Clanwilliam cedars, stands of wagon trees and an array of typical fynbos species.*

PREVIOUS PAGES, LEFT *Although winter brings a blanket of snow and ice, the fertile valleys of Ceres – named in honour of the great Roman goddess of agriculture – encompass many of the country's most productive deciduous fruit farms.*

PREVIOUS PAGES, RIGHT *The vegetation of the typically rocky slopes of Schoemanspoort consists largely of scrub and succulents alternating with cultivated farmlands, which by mid-July are inevitably backed by the snow-covered peaks of the Groot Swartberge.*

LEFT *Located amid the floral splendour of the aptly named Garden Route, the towns of Little Brak and Great Brak (left) take their names, rather ironically, from the brackish river waters around which the settlements were established.*

ABOVE  *The Fancourt Hotel and Country Club on the scenic Garden Route forms the hub of an ever-growing trend in South Africa where swish residential complexes have sprung up along the greens of popular golf courses. Fancourt, with its impressive club facilities and immaculate grounds, has emerged not only as a kingpin on the local golf circuit but also an exclusive enclave of private homes for wealthy golf enthusiasts.*

RIGHT  *The Wilderness landscape on the Garden Route is blessed with abundant rivers, an untramelled woodland and a verdant garden of varied plant life, which makes it not only an essential stopover for casual sightseers, tourists and local holidaymakers, but also a popular drawcard for environmentalists, conservationists and keen adventurers.*

**LEFT**  *Like so many of the little bays and coves that dot the southern Cape coast, Betty's Bay traces its origins to the 1930s when the occasional nature lover, in search of peace and tranquillity, discovered the delights of these out-of-the-way havens and returned again and again to enjoy the solitude offered by a lone stream, a gentle waterfall, and the multitude of wild flowers.*

**ABOVE**  *In stark contrast to the gentle attractions of the many quiet, little getaways sprinkled along the Garden Route, the beaches and resorts of Plettenberg Bay provide a lively and vibrant retreat for vacationers during the height of the popular holiday season.*

**OPPOSITE**  *Nature's Valley, with groves of tall trees covering its gentle mountain slopes, strikes a pleasant balance between the relatively isolated splendour of other small coastal settlements and the energy of vibrant Plettenberg Bay on the Cape's Garden Route.*

# NORTHERN CAPE

*Although the winters of the Northern Cape can be cruel and its desert-like landscape relentless and unforgiving, the veld here is undeniably beautiful, made up of panoramas that incorporate not only uninterrupted views that extend as far as the eye can see, but also stands of thornbush, sandy dunes and the endless expanse of the Great Karoo and Kalahari.*

By far the largest of South Africa's nine provinces, the Northern Cape is a place of wide open spaces and far-flung settlements dotted on a landscape that is simultaneously harsh and surprisingly yielding.

In the northwest is the inhospitable terrain of the semi-desert Kalahari, an expansive stretch of searing red sands that receives a dismally insignificant annual rainfall and yet is home to the indomitable San people.

The semi-desert conditions that comprise the magnificent Great Karoo cover no less than a third of South Africa's total land mass and, thus, a substantial chunk of the southern subcontinent, but its plant life, including the trees that grow in and along the banks of mostly dry riverbeds and much of the vegetation, has evolved through time to withstand the extremes of temperature and aridity. Many of the unique plant species have taken to storing their water requirements in thick leaves and/or bulbous roots, while the seeds of many plants lie dormant for the drier months – and may even

remain so for years – until rains reawaken them and they flower in profusion.

But the arid conditions and pitifully low rainfall also make it ideal not only for sheep farming – and, as a result, the region is one the country's most vital income-producing areas – but also for the extensive diamond mining that takes place here in the alluvial-rich ground.

Kimberley, the provincial capital, traces its very origins to the heady days of the diamond rush that saw insignificant little mining settlements flourish into the burgeoning city, towns and villages we find here today. As a result, the busy streets of the capital form a charming but often confusing network of arbitrary lines reminiscent of its early days when, after a long and tiring trek through the bushveld, fortune-seekers settled on the diamond-bearing kimberlite soils, erecting a haphazard camp of shacks and tents on the dry and dusty land. Thus the town of New Rush became the thriving city of Kimberley, heart of the Northern Cape.

RIGHT *Stretches of the arid Kgalagadi Transfrontier Park, which straddles the Kalahari Gemsbok and the Gemsbok national parks, are covered by the Kalahari soapbush, or driedoring.*

TOP  *No matter how inhospitable the land, domesticated animals of the Kalahari have adapted to make the most of harsh conditions.*

ABOVE  *The Nama* karretjies mense *of Namaqualand, descendants of the pastoralist Khoikhoi, take their colloquial name from the donkey-drawn carts they typically use as transport.*

RIGHT  *Scattered among the province's northernmost expanse of dune and pan is tiny Inkbospan, its camel expeditions offering a less conventional mode of transport.*

LEFT AND BELOW  *As if to counter the marvel of the Great Karoo landscape at the foot of Van Rhyn's Pass (below), the sheltering night skies are ablaze with the southern constellations. It is little wonder, then, that it is here – under a remarkably clear sky – that the Sutherland Observatory (left) was erected.*

BOTTOM AND OPPOSITE  *Like much of the Kalahari, Witsand Nature Reserve – an island of white dunes (bottom) amid a sea of typically red Kalahari sands bleached of its oxides by underground water sources – is dotted with camel thorn trees, home to the characteristic communal nest (opposite) of sociable weavers.*

THIS PAGE  *In an effort to preserve migrating herds of springbok (top left), and the natural habitat of the region's characteristic wildlife such as the Cape fox (left), cheetah (top) and suricate (above), government and conservation officials of have established the Kgalagadi Transfrontier Park, which crosses the border between South Africa and Botswana. This park, which covers an impressive area of more than two million hectares (five million acres) and effectively unites the Kalahari Gemsbok National Park and the Gemsbok National Park, is the continent's first transboundary reserve, and has set the precedent for the establishment of further peace parks.*

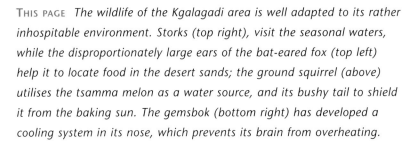

THIS PAGE  *The wildlife of the Kgalagadi area is well adapted to its rather inhospitable environment. Storks (top right), visit the seasonal waters, while the disproportionately large ears of the bat-eared fox (top left) help it to locate food in the desert sands; the ground squirrel (above) utilises the tsamma melon as a water source, and its bushy tail to shield it from the baking sun. The gemsbok (bottom right) has developed a cooling system in its nose, which prevents its brain from overheating.*

OVERLEAF LEFT  *Kamieskroon, in the Sandveld, is ideally suited to the spring-flowering plants for which the region is renowned. In the flowering season between August and October, these rather dour-looking sands burst with blooms, covering the landscape with a blaze of colour.*
OVERLEAF RIGHT  *Vygies of the Mesembryanthemum species are prolific in Namaqualand's Goegap Nature Reserve, and its wild flower garden boasts a fine assembly of nearly 600 plant species.*

LEFT  The halfmens, with its human-like silhouette, is endemic to the Richtersveld and the southwestern regions of Namibia, and holds considerable spiritual significance for the local Nama people.

BELOW  Many of the trails in the Richtersveld date to a time when the region was first settled by farmers and prospectors, but the De Hoop camp site in the Orange River Valley caters for the latter-day adventurer.

ABOVE AND OPPOSITE TOP  Although the flood waters of the Augrabies Falls (above), which takes its name from the Khoikhoi word meaning 'place of great noise', is an impressive sight, the desert-like landscape (opposite top) through which the river flows is dry and rocky.

OPPOSITE BOTTOM  Apart from the occasional camp site, there are few indications of human habitation in the Richtersveld National Park and the only signs of life on the rocky landscape are rare endemic plants.

8

9

10

1

12

# CREEPY CRAWLIES

Of all the reptiles, spiders, scorpions, insects and crustaceans endemic to the desert sands, scrubland, marshes and bushveld of South Africa, only a very small percentage are poisonous and an even smaller number pose any danger to humankind. South Africa, nevertheless, boasts a huge number of these creepy crawlies: there are some 400 reptile species, of which 140 are snakes, and only 20 are dangerous; about 5 000 species of arachnids – which includes among its numbers some 175 species and subspecies of scorpions; and more than 100 000 species of insects – the world's most prolific creatures – of every shape, size and description.
(1) blue-headed agama, (2) gaboon adder, (3) marsh crab, (4) Buthus scorpion, (5) praying mantis, (6) citrus swallowtail butterfly, (7) Uroplectes scorpion, (8) Natal Midlands dwarf chameleon, (9) horned baboon spider, (10) Cape cobra, (11) Nile (water) monitor, (12) green tree frog, (13) scarab beetle.

13

# EASTERN CAPE

*In a world of golden beaches set against thickets of dense bush and a gentle hinterland of green hills interlaced with winding rivers and dotted with tranquil lakes, the Eastern Cape is thoroughly enchanting, its delightful little settlements but highlights of a landscape that is largely rural and temperate in nature and mood.*

Steeped as it is in a history that is as rich and varied as its landscape, the Eastern Cape is a land of endless stretches of hilly terrain, rolling dunes, and a rugged coast battered by the volatile nature of the ocean. The towns and villages – and even the two cities, Port Elizabeth and East London – find their roots in the rural settlements established either as colonial towns in the nineteenth century or even earlier, in the times when small Xhosa-speaking communities began to settle the hills and valleys of what is today the Eastern Cape Province. A hotbed of militant struggle during the apartheid years and the fight for democracy, the innate pride and independent nature of these people has meant that the province has since seen much transformation in modern times, but is essentially still a rather unexplored corner of South Africa, surprisingly unaffected by the general upturn in tourism witnessed by the rest of the country.

Despite this apparent contradiction, however, there is much to see and marvel at in the multifaceted landscape of the Eastern Cape. The cities of Port Elizabeth and East London, leaders in the economy of the region, are lined with gracious old buildings dating back to their colonial past, while much of the hinterland is interspersed with the traditional homesteads of the rural Xhosa people.

In pride of place, too, is the popular Addo Elephant National Park, home to a population of some 300 African elephants and small herds of red hartebeest, kudu and even black rhino.

This malaria-free veld is also home to a number of small but promising game reserves and conservation areas, such as the Mkambati Nature Reserve on its northern coast, settled by a fascinating array of wildlife. The game-watching experience in these reserves may be very different to the wildlife safaris offered by the game-rich areas of the country's northern stretches, but the unique flavour of luxury, combined with the wildness of the Eastern Cape veld, make it one of the region's most rewarding excursions.

RIGHT *Many of the hills of the Eastern Cape's distinctly rural landscape are dotted with traditional homesteads of the Xhosa people.*

**ABOVE** *The mouth of the mighty Kei River acts as the southernmost boundary of the Eastern Cape's scenic Wild Coast, a lush and ruggedly beautiful expanse of coast that reaches as far north as the Mtamvuna River.*

**LEFT** *In the heart of the marine wonderland that is the Wild Coast lies the region's largest nature reserve, Mkambati, which is bound in the north by the waters of the Mtentu River.*

RIGHT  *Even in the days when the Wild Coast lay within the confines of the Transkei, its scenic beauty and untamed coastline was a haven for adventurers such as the naturalists who ride along its exceptional beaches. Given the tempestuous nature of the ocean on this somewhat precarious stretch of coast, the notoriously volatile shore has seen many a ship flounder here throughout history.*

TOP  *The Nahoon River, near East London, is but one of a significant number of small water courses that wind their way through the Eastern Cape interior toward the Atlantic.*

ABOVE  *East London is the Eastern Cape's second largest city, and – situated as it is at the mouth of the Buffalo River – serves as the country's only river harbour.*

RIGHT  *The city of East London – although relatively small in comparison to South Africa's major metropolitan centres – has seen considerable growth in recent years, most notably the exciting Latimer's Landing waterfront development.*

LEFT AND BELOW  *Port Elizabeth, named in honour of the late wife of acting governor Sir Rufane Donkin in 1820, is South Africa's fifth largest city and, although once the hub of the country's vehicle-manufacturing industry, has capitalised rather on its resort attractions, proclaiming itself the 'friendly city'. Chief among its drawcards is the popular Museum Complex and Oceanarium on Marine Drive. The performing seals (left) and bottlenose dolphins (below) are all bred in captivity and are not replaced with captured specimens when they die.*

OPPOSITE  *Notwithstanding the fact that Port Elizabeth remains South Africa's third largest port and, as such, a vital cog in the country's industry-driven economy, the waters of Algoa Bay – a name it has retained since its settler origins – have remained an equally important playground for sailing enthusiasts.*

ABOVE *Eastern Cape architecture is based largely on the region's colonial ties, as is evident in the elaborate facade of East London's Ann Bryant Gallery.*
BELOW *The spire of Grahamstown's Anglican Cathedral of St Michael & St George, towering more than 50 metres (165 feet), is the focal point of the university town, known affectionately, too, as the City of Angels.*

ABOVE  *Cradock's Dutch Reformed Church was, somewhat ironically for a Dutch church serving an Afrikaans-speaking congregation, modelled on London's famed St-Martin's-in-the-Field.*

BELOW  *The grand Edwardian facade of Port Elizabeth's appropriately named Edward Hotel is one of the city's best-preserved historical buildings.*

TOP  *Swartvlei, the deepest and most extensive lake on the entire Garden Route – which, according to formal boundaries, ends at the mouth of the Storms River in the Eastern Cape – was formed when the valley filled with water as sea levels rose following the Ice Age.*

ABOVE  *With the abundance of water sources in the Tsitsikamma area, it is little wonder that its rivers, including the Storms River in the heart of the reserve, have carved deep gorges from the verdant landscape.*

RIGHT  *Enjoying an annual rainfall of more than 1 200 millimetres (48 inches), Tsitsikamma is laced with a number of streams and rivers, including the Groot River, which forms its western boundary.*

ABOVE *Following concerted efforts by conservationists, the once endangered Cape mountain zebra – with its distinctive 'grid-iron' rump pattern – is now a prominent inhabitant of the Mountain Zebra National Park, but the reserve also plays host to a number of other mammals, including eland, springbok and black wildebeest and over 200 bird species, such as martial eagles, chanting goshawks and Cape eagle owls.*

ABOVE *The Mountain Zebra National Park, some 25 kilometres (16 miles) south of the town of Cradock, is situated in a natural basin at the foot of the Coetzeesberge in the Eastern Cape interior. Established in 1937 to help preserve the zebra population from which it takes its name, today the park covers some 6 500 hectares (16 000 acres), which includes a demanding but not too challenging three-day hiking trail.*

LEFT AND ABOVE *Protruding from the rugged plains of the southern regions of the Great Karoo are the rock formations that form the craggy face of the Valley of Desolation, exposed over the centuries by the corrosive action of the wind-blown sands, leaving behind only the hardened dolerite resistent to erosion. In the colonial days of exploration into the hinterland, these towering rock spires demarcated the furthest boundaries of the frontier and the nearby town of Graaff-Reinet, established in the early nineteenth century, is still a thriving settlement.*
OPPOSITE *The mountains that encircle the small town of Barkly East are dotted with glaciated pavements, dolerite kopjes, prehistoric rock formations, and treacherous mountain passes, and yet this apparently formidable landscape is popular with both hikers – there are a number of acclaimed trails in the region – and mountain bikers.*

# KwaZulu-Natal

*A trek through KwaZulu-Natal is an inspirational meander across
a landscape of remarkable contrasts, from the golden dunes and sands
of its magnificent coast to the bounteous knolls, mountains and lush valleys
of the Midlands – in many ways, one of the most spectacular stretches
of this otherwise semiarid subcontinent.*

Vast tracts of KwaZulu-Natal, the ancestral home of the Zulu nation, are blessed with an abundant rainfall, making for an Eden of rolling hills and wild open spaces that stretches from the magnificent Drakensberg of the Great Escarpment to the splendour of the gentle sands that line its shore.

Adorned with an intriguing blend of the rural and urban, the province is one of South Africa's most picturesque, its modern and vibrant cityscapes a perfect match for the dazzling countryside beyond that marks the craggy rise of the great Drakensberg. This 'Mountain of the Dragon' is undeniably the most significant – and spectacular – of the great heights of the Escarpment, its age-old rockfaces dotted with caves painted in the imaginative style of ancient San rock artists.

Both the principal centres of Durban and Pietermaritzburg, established as little more than colonial outposts in the early days of European settlement, are today modern cities of centuries-old facades and contemporary architecture, their streets lined with a fine collection of timeless structures reminiscent of their colourful past.

Covered with glades of indigenous trees and carpets of wild flowers, the interior also forms the backdrop to some of the country's most magnificent natural wonders. Of the many spectacles of KwaZulu-Natal – from its pristine beaches to the craggy inclines of the Drakensberg – one of the most extraordinary vistas must be the eerie expanse that is the setting of the legendary Valley of a Thousand Hills, an undulating sweep of gradients steeped in a turbulent history of long-fought battles and wars braved by tribal warriors.

Rich in a variety of indigenous flora and fauna, KwaZulu-Natal also boasts a selection of outstanding national parks and conservation areas. Supreme among these are the Hluhluwe-Umfolozi Park – an untamed wilderness grazed by zebra, buffalo and white rhino – and the enormous biodiversity of the Greater St Lucia Wetland Park, extremely sensitive to human intervention of any kind.

RIGHT *The Mont-aux-Sources Amphitheatre towers over the valleys of the Drakensberg's Royal Natal National Park.*

TOP  *As one of the southern subcontinent's busiest ports, Durban is South Africa's largest harbour and thus an important industrial hub through which much of the country's crops and mining minerals pass en route to foreign shores.*

ABOVE AND RIGHT  *Although the balmy city of Durban is KwaZulu-Natal's largest, it is not the provincial capital; that honour is reserved for Pietermaritzburg. Nevertheless, Durban is the country's third largest city, and much of the leisure activity for which the holiday mecca is famed is centred around its yacht basin (above) and splendid beachfront (right).*

LEFT  *With its hot summers and balmy, temperate winters, the coastline of KwaZulu-Natal – South Africa's 'Garden Province' – is a holiday mecca virtually throughout the year. In December, however, the holiday season is at its peak, with resorts, such as those at Margate on the South Coast, bursting with visitors to its palm-lined beaches.*
BOTTOM LEFT AND ABOVE  *Proudly referred to as the Golden Mile, Durban's beachfront (above) is a conglomeration of fashionable nightspots, lively bistros and endless beaches packed with cheerful holidaymakers, surfers and rollerbladers attracted by popular drawcards such as Water World (bottom left) and the pedestrian walkways of neon-lit Marine Parade.*
OPPOSITE  *The warm Indian Ocean that laps the golden sands of the temperate coastal strip north of Durban is lined with a series of holiday apartments, hotel complexes and timeshare resorts that have earned Umhlanga Rocks a reputation as one of KwaZulu-Natal's finest holiday destinations, every bit as enjoyable but considerably less glitzy than those on the South Coast.*

ABOVE  *Steeped as it is in such a diverse cultural and social history influenced much by the Eastern heritage of many of its people, the Durban cityscape is punctuated with the elaborately turreted mosques of the Muslim community.*

ABOVE AND OPPOSITE  *Durban's Temple of Understanding, its interior reverberating with sacred chant and the spires of its ultramodern exterior reaching heavenward, is an important centre of worship for followers of Krishna.*

TOP  *Whereas many of KwaZulu-Natal's favoured tourist hotspots focus on the safari experience, the cultural village of Shakaland on the outskirts of Eshowe offers a fascinating alternative – a glimpse into the age-old customs and traditions of its indigenous Zulu people.*

ABOVE  *Situated on a tiny peninsula banked by the Black Mfolozi River in the Hluhluwe-Umfolozi Park, Gqoyeni Bush Lodge presents some of the best game-viewing the region has to offer.*

RIGHT  *At home in the nearly 36 000 hectares (90 000 acres) of low-lying thornveld that comprise the Mkuzi Game Reserve in the shadow of the Ubombo Mountains are herds of blue wildebeest, Burchell's zebra and a spectacular array of other game.*

THIS PAGE  *The lush landscape of KwaZulu-Natal offers a very different view of the more conventional acacia-dotted image of the Dark Continent, and its clinging heat provides an idyllic environment for tropical plant species such as the orchids (left) and fragrant frangipanis (below and bottom) featured in Durban's Botanical Garden.*
OPPOSITE TOP AND BOTTOM  *The legacy of Durban owes as much to the heritage of the East as it does to the region's temperate climes, and Indian wedding guests at Durban's Botanical Garden (top) and the contrasting image of the city's Japanese Gardens (bottom) add much to this complex face of Africa.*

**OPPOSITE TOP AND ABOVE** *Although they represent the furthest extremes of the coastal belt of KwaZulu-Natal, the Umtamvuna River mouth (opposite top) at Port Edward – the southernmost limit – and Kosi Bay (above) – in the far north, offer much the same vistas of a tropical landscape washed by the warm waters of the Atlantic.*

**OPPOSITE BOTTOM** *Adjacent to the St Lucia Marine Reserve, Sodwana Bay is extremely popular among divers – for its exceptional wealth of corals, reefs and other underwater marine life – and sightseers, who wonder at the scenic natural beauty of a region.*

**RIGHT** *Along with the vleis and marshlands of Lake St Lucia, the St Lucia and Maputaland marine reserves and the Coastal Forest Reserve, picturesque Kosi Bay forms part of the 250 000-hectare (620 000 acres) Greater St Lucia Wetland Park. This spectacular panorama, ever under the threat of human encroachment, comprises a vast range of habitats, from sensitive marine ecosystems and coastal forests to salt- and freshwater marshes, estuaries and luxuriant tropical plains.*

TOP AND RIGHT  *The western extreme of the province is demarcated by a wall of crests that makes up the KwaZulu-Natal Drakensberg, which separates it from the mountain kingdom of Lesotho beyond. One of the most spectacular of these towering ridges is Cathedral Peak, the valleys of its foothills coursing with streams and rivers, such as the iNtonyelana eMpumalanga (top) and eMweni (right).*

ABOVE  *The Cobham State Forest and nature reserve act as a catchment area for the Mzimkhulu River and its tributaries, and the untamed expanse of this pristine wilderness provides ideal terrain in which to explore the Southern Drakensberg region.*

LEFT *The highlying regions of KwaZulu-Natal and the Drakensberg are studded with some of the country's finest natural reserves and mountain wilderness, prime among them the magnificent gorges and grasslands of the Royal Natal National Park, famed more for its spectacular scenery and popular hiking trails than for its selection of big-game species.*
ABOVE AND OPPOSITE LEFT *Although trout is not a fish indigenous to southern African waters, trout-fishing has become one of KwaZulu-Natal's most popular pastimes since the fish was introduced into the Mooi River in 1890. Today, the well-stocked trout dams in and around Kamberg – famed too for the indigenous rock art at Game Pass Shelter – attract many enthusiastic fly-fishermen.*

RIGHT  *The spectacular Howick Falls on the equally impressive Mgeni River are known locally as kwaNogqasa, which means 'place of the tall one'. The falls tumble some 95 metres (310 feet) into the 660 hectare (160 acres) Umgeni Valley Nature Reserve, a protected haven for a variety of wildlife, including antelope and bird species, and even giraffe.*
OVERLEAF  *In stark contrast to the vision of sparkling waters gushing down and through the rocky gorges of KwaZulu-Natal in the summer rainfall season, the winter landscape of the Drakensberg is a world of opposites as a blanket of snow descends on towns such as Nottingham Road (left) and Himeville (right), which dot the foothills of the Great Escarpment.*

# FREE STATE

*The stark beauty of the Free State is a kaleidoscope of changing colours
and a myriad spectacular panoramas – all of them different, from stretches
of the searing savanna, through green farmland to the simplicity
of the many charming mining settlements sprinkled across the mesmerising
veld that lines its winding roads.*

With the magnificent splendour of its cityscapes, the pastel shades of its open fields and the changing faces of its many people, the sunny wilderness of the Free State is endowed with a warmth and simplicty seen nowhere else in South Africa. Vast vistas of gravel plains strewn with boulders and rocks, sandy veld dotted with shrubs and occasionally sprinkled with colourful fields of wild flowers lend this gentle but enigmatic region a beauty that is all its own.

On close inspection, the Free State is remarkably attractive, with many of its inhabitants – floral, faunal and human – having adapted remarkably well to the often-harsh realities of the landscape. The land here, in parts planted with productive farmland and in others pinpointed with evidence of the province's considerable mining interests, is dominated by the city of Bloemfontein – the confluence of no less than six major routes that criss-cross South Africa and quite literally the heart of the country. Although its origins may have been

simple indeed – the name means 'flower fountain' and is taken from the spring at which weary travellers stopped on their way through the dusty interior – this city, the provincial capital and seat of the country's judiciary, is vastly underrated as a gem of the hinterland. Originally established, quite ironically, as a British military stronghold in the interior, for many, many years Bloemfontein was a centre of Afrikaner independence and today many of its grand historical buildings are monuments to the region's often troubled history. The city, towns and villages of the Free State – with their churches and museums, galleries and memorials – are fringed not only by the rugged landscape so characteristic of the region, but also a series of relatively small reserves and parks dedicated to the preservation of the surrounding veld and the numerous plant and animal species that inhabit it.

Seldom acknowledged for its remarkable beauty, the Free State countryside is indeed a tribute to the natural splendour of South Africa.

RIGHT *Taking pride of place among the Free State's protected reserves is the scenic wonderland of the Golden Gate Highlands National Park.*

OPPOSITE *The sandstone outcrops, meandering rivers and horizonless expanse of the Free State wilderness around Clarens provide an ideal landscape for the pony-trekking adventures offered by the local Basotho, renowned for their skilled horsemanship. The Basotho pony is a descendant of the Javanese pack horse introduced into the region in colonial times, and is the rural population's most important mode of transport.*

ABOVE AND RIGHT *The proximity of the Free State to Lesotho, the traditional home of the Basotho people – which forms part of the province's eastern boundary, inevitably means that many of the Basotho are perfectly at home in the Free State. The Basotho Cultural Village, a 'living' museum of traditional homesteads in the Qwa-Qwa National Park, honours the cultural and social contribution of the Sotho nation to the history of both the province and South African.*

LEFT AND TOP *Although studded with groves of montane vegetation (left) and the occasional stream, the Golden Gate Highlands National Park is perhaps best known for the dramatic sandstone rockfaces (top) that characterise its landscape.*

ABOVE *The mountain slopes and grassy hills that cover Golden Gate – itself part of the Drakensberg escarpment – are grazed by antelope species such as springbok, wildebeest, blesbok, and small herds of grey rhebok (above).*

OPPOSITE *The sandstone promontory of Golden Gate's landmark Sentinel, standing guard over the picturesque valley of the Little Caledon River, is the most recognisable of the park's many craggy cliff faces.*

**LEFT** *The rural landscape of Clarens, situated just north of the Lesotho border, is a wonderland of open veld and golden grassland skirted by a series of rocky ridges.*

**BELOW** *Brightly painted rondavels, decorated in typical Basotho fashion, form part of the visitors' accommodation at Glen Reenen, one of only two rest camps serving Golden Gate; the other is Brandwag, to the west.*

**OPPOSITE** *Although the Free State is very much an agicultural centre, with much of the land given over to cultivated fields of grain and other vital crops, the picturesque quality of areas such as Fouriesburg add much to its rugged scenic beauty.*

**OVERLEAF** *Because the rainfall of the province is generally low and the flow of its rivers is thus largely seasonal, the Free State's water requirements – most notably for its agricultural lands – need to be supplemented by the waters trapped by man-made dams, such as Meulspruit (left) near Ficksburg and the Allemanskraal Dam (right) in the Willem Pretorius Game Reserve to the northwest.*

TOP, CENTRE AND ABOVE  *Of all the many faces of the Free State, the most recognisable must be its wild cosmos, the delicate pink, white and mauve blooms flourishing in open fields, along busy highways and high on the province's hilly slopes.*

RIGHT  *While the beautiful cosmos is essentially a weed that grows wildly across much of the province, the Free State remains largely a land of cultivated fields, producing no less than a third of the country's grain harvest.*

2

4

6

# RAINBOW NATION

n a nation that boasts 11 official languages and a multitude of localised
dialects dispersed across a population of about 45 million, it is little wonder
that the rich tapestry of cultural influence has contributed much to the
exciting diversity of this land. Generally speaking, most black South Africans
trace their origins to one of four broad groups, two of which may again be
separated into smaller ethnic groups. The Nguni people, for example, comprise
the Zulu, Xhosa, Swazi and Ndebele nations, while the Sotho consist of the
Tswana, North Sotho and South Sotho (generally referred to as the Basotho).
The Shangaan-Tsonga and Venda people comprise individual groups with no
affiliation to either the Nguni or Sotho. Nevertheless, the timelessness of ritual,
the complexity of language, and the inherent skill reflected in indigenous craft
are all integral to traditional South African culture.

(1) Zulu warriors, (2) Zulu bride, (3) Ndebele family, (4) Basotho man,
(5) Xhosa matron, (6) Zulu maidens, or intombi, (7) San hunters, (8) Tonga
sangoma, (9) Zulu sangoma, (10) Venda musicians at the Python Dance,
(11) Pondo, (12) traditional crafts.

# NORTH WEST

*Although sweltering and apparently desolate in appearance,
the North West Province is a picture of near-desert sands in the far west,
open African bushveld in the central region and rocky mountainscape
in the far north – all of which are home to small pockets
of predominantly rural communities.*

The summer rainfall and bushveld vegetation of the North West lends it a unique beauty, highlighted by a vast range of landscapes, from the buttresses of the Magaliesberg and Pilanesberg to the dusty reaches of its northernmost plains that border Botswana.

The region's early pioneers encountered in this place of untrammelled solitude many of the wild animals that have today become the province's most important assets. These initial explorers set about establishing small settlements in this wilderness, but were, of course, completely unaware that a thriving tourism industry – consisting of safari-goers, sightseers and wildlife photographers – would mushroom around the rough tracks carved into the landscape by their cattle, pack oxen and simple wagons. Today, many of the rural inhabitants continue to live the life of the ancients in villages that speckle the terrain, and it is this simple life that contributed to the rather unique flavour of the region.

Temperatures and humidity here are high, giving rise to prosperous mixed-farming endeavours that include field crops, such as wheat, and the extensive cattle-ranching that makes the region one of South Africa's top beef and dairy centres. Also dotted along this varied landscape is a series of small, privately owned game farms, which owe much of their success to the substantial herds of animals that originally established themselves in the region in a forgotten era and, in more recent years, have been successfully reintroduced to the area.

Although many of the human settlements are small and somewhat insignificant to the tourism industry so important to many of the more traditionally picturesque regions of the country, the North West boasts the most ambitious visitors' drawcard of the South African interior: the unparalleled magic of Sun City and the majestic Palace of the Lost City in the heart of the Pilanesberg, attributes that have transformed this previously unexplored region into a wonderland of diversity.

RIGHT *Intrepid sightseers set off in hot-air balloons to marvel over the Magaliesberg in the North West Province.*

ABOVE *One of the first important water development projects established on the Highveld, Hartbeespoort Dam is today also a popular resort.*
BELOW *The waters of the Olifantsnek Dam, between the Magaliesberg towns of Rustenburg and Magaliesburg, provide a welcome respite in the region's hot bush- and thornveld.*

ABOVE  *The waters of Hartbeespoort Dam, fed by the Crocodile and Magalies rivers, are vital to Johannesburg's water supply and irrigation of tracts of cultivated land in the area.*

BELOW  *Visitors' facilities of the popular Schoemansville settlement on the shores of the reservoir epitomise the resort-like character of Hartbeespoort.*

TOP  Among the Lost City's many man-made elements, constructed to appear as if they had only recently been rediscovered after centuries of neglect, are the honey-coloured foundations of the Elephant footbridge.

ABOVE CENTRE  No matter which of the 18 holes you are playing on the splendid 55-hectare (136 acres) golf course designed by Gary Player, always in sight are the magical facades of the Lost City complex.

ABOVE  The 'wildness' of Sun City's Kwena Gardens Crocodile Farm is a far cry from the lights and sirens of the slot-machines just metres away.

RIGHT  Rising high above the thorn trees and rocky contours of the Pilanesberg stands the mythical Palace of the Lost City, its crystal domes covering a labyrinth of marbled corridors, sweeping staircases and a series of breathtaking chambers that comprise the grand hotel.

**BELOW AND OPPOSITE** *In the middle of an otherwise barren and unaccommodating landscape, the Wave Pool in the Lost City's legendary Valley of the Waves – hidden amid the dry African veld and miles and miles from the waters and shores of the nearest ocean – is a 'coastal' paradise of rolling seas, blue bays and Caribbean-style beaches. Created entirely by modern technology, the seascape is one of the complex's most alluring features.*

**ABOVE** *Legend has it that, in a time long ago, peace-loving nomads stumbled across this isolated Highveld valley, and here they built their unparalleled kingdom of splendour. For hundreds of years they tended its grounds and nurtured its landscape – until a devastating earthquake destroyed everything. Today, the thunder and smoke caused by that cataclysmic earthquake is periodically recreated at the Lost City.*

1

2

3

4

5

6

7

8

9

10

11

12

13

14

15

16

17

18

19

20

21

# AVIAN JEWELS

*Given the enormous variation in vegetation types, the forests, savannas, grasslands, coastal plains and montane and riverine habitats of South Africa are blessed with over 900 bird species.*
*(1) ground woodpecker, (2) Cape rock thrush, (3) lilac-breasted roller, (4) crowned crane,*
*(5) Burchell's coucal, (6) blue waxbill, (7) crested barbet, (8) greater honeyguide,*
*(9) pied kingfisher, (10) carmine bee-eater, (11) spurwinged goose, (12) lanner falcon,*
*(13) African black oystercatcher, (14) purple gallinule, (15) yellowbilled duck, (16) squacco heron,*
*(17) swallowtailed bee-eater, (18) pygmy goose, (19) giant kingfisher, (20) brownheaded parrot,*
*(21) blue crane, (22) malachite sunbird.*

22

# GAUTENG

*From the great urban sprawls to the vast openness of the Highveld, Gauteng is rich in every sense, counting among its many treasures the exhaustive gold deposits of the Witwatersrand, the vibrancy of local cultures and the eclectic composition of its varied landscape, a world of commerce and industry comfortably embraced by a vast countryside.*

Everything in Gauteng, or so it seems, is bigger and better. The wealthiest and most populated of the nine provinces, Gauteng boasts a population of some 7 million, who together produce about 40 per cent of South Africa's gross national product. Widely acclaimed as the site of one of the world's richest gold deposits, not for nothing is the principal city of Johannesburg known as the City of Gold, 600 tons of which are mined here in a single year – some 35 per cent of the world's total. Much of the mining activity is focused on the Witwatersrand – meaning 'white water ridge' – home, too, to great centres of finance and fine art, museums and mine dumps. And at the centre of this magnificent Highveld are the impressive proportions of Johannesburg, the 'New York of Africa', famed for its fine assembly of universities, art galleries, world-class restaurants and music venues.

The unusual blend of cultures, from theatres to shanty towns, is a far cry from the tiny mining camp established on the dusty veld in the early nineteenth century. It is here, along the stony ridges and gold-rich soils, that Australian prospector George Harrison first discovered the precious metal that was to become the mainstay of the South African economy and on which the great city was built. Today, on this very same soil stands the Johannesburg Securities Exchange and everything that it has come to represent in this economic hub of South Africa.

But there is much more to Gauteng than the great cities of Johannesburg and Pretoria, in themselves surprisingly green, especially following the summer rains. The lakes and dams that dot their outskirts have long been favoured by pleasure seekers as weekend retreats and welcome hideaways, and contribute much to the extraordinary dynamic of Gauteng. Both Johannesburg and Pretoria are surrounded by a game-rich countryside that boasts a number of reserves and parklands, which have gained an enviable reputation for the diversity of wildlife and contrasting panoramas.

RIGHT *Watched over by the Hillbrow Tower, the lights of South Africa's leading city begin to twinkle as night settles over Johannesburg.*

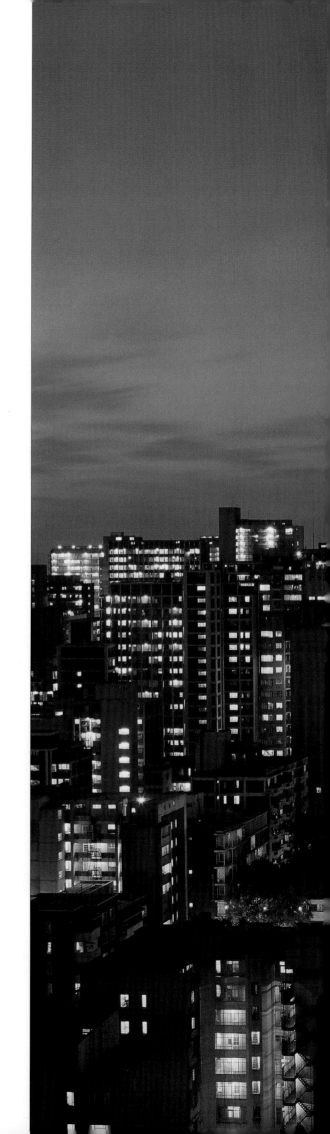

ABOVE  *Forming part of the Braamfontein Spruit (stream), Emmarentia Dam, in Jan van Riebeeck Park adjoining the Johannesburg Botanical Garden, is a popular getaway much favoured by weekend sailors.*

ABOVE *The focus of the Randburg Waterfront, the 'harbour' complex in the heart of landlocked Gauteng, is on its man-made lake and the shops, restaurants and entertainment venues that crowd its banks.*

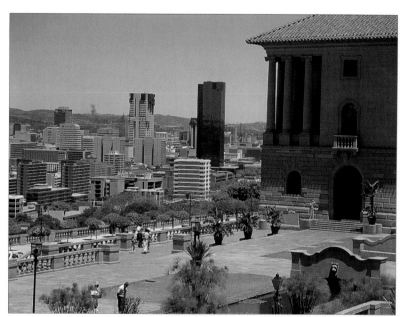

THIS PAGE *Located in the temperate valley of the Apies River, the Jacaranda City of Pretoria has served virtually throughout its existence as a capital – of the old Boer Republic of the Transvaal and, in more recent years, as the administrative capital of South Africa. Today, it remains a seat of national, provincial and civic power – the latter based largely at City Hall (above).*

OPPOSITE TOP *Sprawled at the foot of the Union Buildings are its meticulously manicured lawns and garden, which offer superlative views of the city, a veritable jungle of modern structures.*

OPPOSITE BOTTOM *Conceived in neoclassical style by the creative genius of Sir Herbert Baker, South Africa's most prolific architect of the time, the Union Buildings were erected – in 1913 – in an amphitheatre formation.*

TOP LEFT   *The historic Dolobran building in Parktown is a fantasy of gables, domes, crests and stained glass, designed – not by Sir Herbert Baker, who was originally commissioned to design the building, but by J.A. Cope Christie – in what is loosely described as Colonial Queen Ann Revival style.*

LEFT   *Reminiscent, in parts, of the South African colonial style of yesteryear, the Village Walk shopping mall in Sandton is a recent addition to the Johannesburg skyline.*

BOTTOM LEFT   *The modern Montecasino entertainment complex, casino and hotel in Fourways draws on the varied Tuscan and Victorian influences of the city's older structures.*

ABOVE   *Although the high ceilings and gleaming wooden floors of the Johannesburg Art Gallery are distinct reminders of the early origins of the building, its light and airy interior gives it a more contemporary look.*

OPPOSITE TOP   *The casino at Gold Reef City, an animated recreation of old Johannesburg, was reconstructed in typical period style of the nineteenth century, reflecting the face of the city as it was during the early gold-mining days.*

OPPOSITE BOTTOM   *Following a popular trend that has taken root throughout much of the country, Johannesburg's vast Caesar's Palace hotel and casino complex was built in a grand, opulent style prompted by the designs of colonial Africa.*

# NORTHERN PROVINCE

*From a land where much of its wilderness is parched by the African sun rises a scenic beauty that is, although in places rather stark and occasionally unforgiving, quite breathtaking in its bushveld simplicity. These northern stretches of South Africa, alive with the colour and sounds of Africa, are a delight of texture and temperament.*

In contrast to the great urban settlements of Gauteng, the landscape of the Northern Province is wild and, to a large degree, relatively empty of people, absorbing much of its character from its undisputed rustic beauty. Dry and dusty plains give way to tracts of grassland interspersed with acacia and camel thorn, the eastern boundary delineated by the northern reaches of the impressive expanse that is the Kruger National Park, a wonderland of wildlife the Northern Province shares with its southern neighbour, Mpumalanga.

It is from the Northern Province that the expansive Lowveld stretches south into the interior in a wild sweep of bushveld haunted by the eerie call of the fish eagle. This land, originally the exclusive terrain of big-game hunters and pioneers, intrepid adventurers and explorers, is today the home of the country's most recognised game species and a safari destination for hundreds of thousands of visitors travelling to the region's world-acclaimed reserves. Whether it is following

the tracks of a pride of lions, watching the fascinating aerial parade of bird life from the seclusion of a hide, or dining in the luxury of exclusive retreats, the open country and primal wilderness are filled to the brim with big game and other extraordinary wildlife of Africa.

A series of seasonal rivers and streams – a rare resource indeed in a countryside largely deprived of reliable rainfall – brings life to this bare scrubland and undulating grassland, acacia stands and groves of thornbush studding the veld with evidence of a rich and varied plant life that ranges from the smallest of blooms to the tallest of mighty baobabs.

This game- and flora-rich region in the northeast of South Africa boasts some of the finest natural resources in the country, and South African conservation authorities, on both a national and provincial level, have employed a host of tried and proven methods in the continuing fight to save what remains of the natural heritage of the country, and particularly that of its precious northern provinces.

RIGHT *Lake Funduzi has enormous spiritual significance for the local Venda people of the northern provinces of South Africa.*

TOP *Originally little more than a simple agricultural research centre, the town of Tzaneen, with its high rainfall and rich soils, has today become synonymous with tropical produce, such as avocado pears.*
ABOVE *Plantations of citrus fruit, such as oranges, stand side by side with the forests of the densely wooded Tzaneen district.*
RIGHT *The agricultural economy of the Northern Province relies heavily on the tea industry, and much of the green countryside around Tzaneen is covered with tea plantations, the fragrant leaves harvested in spring and summer.*

**OPPOSITE** *In a region renowned for its extensive orchards and plantations rather than its obvious tourist potential, the small towns and villages north of Pietersburg are nevertheless filled with simple delights, such as Haenertsburg Spring Fair and annual Cherry Blossom Festival – an arts-and-crafts jamboree that coincides with the harvest of the commercially grown cherries.*

**ABOVE** *The heat and humidity of the Northern Province mean that areas such as Haenertsburg are not only thickly wooded, but also a floral paradise in which flowers such as the azaleas cultivated here flourish.* **RIGHT** *Tzaneen, Haenertsburg and the surrounding hamlets are famed for the spring-flowering season of both azaleas and cherries.*

Top *The forest of giant cycads on the slopes above the royal kraal of the Rain Queen, Modjadji, forms the spiritual heart of the matriarchal kingdom of the Lobedu people. Of the nearly 30 species in South Africa, these sacred cycads are the tallest, reaching a height of some 13 metres (42 feet).*

Above *Located in a region steeped in the mythology of its local people, the woodlands of Magoebaskloof once sheltered the rebel Tlou chief Makgoba who, refusing to supplement the tax coffers of the Transvaal Republic, was hunted down and killed here by Swazi warriors.*

Right *The strictly guarded wilderness area of the Wolkberg is a 22 000-hectare (54 000 acres) mountainscape dotted with tranquil pools and scattered with a wildlife population of reedbuck, duiker, springbok and the occasional leopard. Its rugged isolation also means that it is popular hiking terrain.*

ABOVE  *Undisputed heartland of South Africa's extraordinary diversity of wildlife, the Kruger National Park – which straddles the borders of the Northern Province and adjacent Mpumalanga – is a haven of big game, including buffalo, considered by many to be the most dangerous of the Big Five, seen here drinking at the park's Kumana water hole.*

OPPOSITE  *The Moholoholo Rehabilitation Centre at Hoedspruit, just west of the Klaserie Nature Reserve within the boundaries of Kruger, is but one of a number of conservation efforts that have been established in the area to rehabilitate orphaned wildlife in the region.*

OVERLEAF, TOP LEFT  *Apart from its prolific wildlife species, the Northern Province is also the ancestral home of many of southern Africa's indigenous people, and archaeologists based in the Kruger National Park have unearthed a wealth of ancient artefacts, including ceramics and hand tools, crafted by early civilisations.*

OVERLEAF, CENTRE  *Archaeological discoveries at the now partly restored ruins at Albasini, near Kruger's Pretoriuskop camp, have offered a fascinating insight into the fiefdom  of João Albasini – a Portuguese-Italian hunter and trader who settled here in the mid-1800s – that included exiled members of local Shangaan communities.*

OVERLEAF, BOTTOM LEFT  *Many of the ancient sites unearthed across the Northern Province have revealed some fascinating finds, among them a number of Stone Age implements, including a scraper and hand axe dating back to some one million years ago.*

OVERLEAF, RIGHT  *Intricately crafted gold artefacts, discovered among the baobab-lined, stone-walled ruins of the Thulamela Royal Village, suggests evidence of a relatively sophisticated society in which the precious metal must have been mined and processed to craft the royal jewels found on the ancient site.*

1

2

3

4

# IN THE WILD

*The enormous diversity and range of the South African landscape has ensured that the region is home to one of the world's greatest panoramas of wildlife. More than 1 000 mammal species occur on the continent and more than 300 of these can be found in the wilds and in the country's 17 national parks and more than 500 smaller conservation areas. South Africa's big cats, primates, rodents, carnivores, antelope, and other mammal species – among them the much-photographed Big Five of lion, leopard, elephant, rhino (both black and white) and buffalo – have proven to be the subcontinent's most enduring drawcards, attracting the attention of conservationists, photographers, tourists and sightseers to the bushveld, grasslands and savannas of South Africa.*

6

7

8

9

With more than more than three million hectares of its total land area devoted almost exclusively to the preservation of indigenous flora and fauna, South Africa boasts one of the world's most impressive conservation records, and certainly one of the most comprehensive wildlife management systems on the continent. The intrinsically wild character of the land has also given rise to one of Africa's most impressive national parks, acclaimed worldwide for the sound principles adopted by its custodians in the management of its wildlife resources. The Kruger National Park is home to some 500 bird and 100 reptile species, 33 amphibians, 49 freshwater fish and, at about 147 species, nearly half of the national complement of mammals.

(1) wild dog, (2) king cheetah, (3) hippopotamus, (4) sable, (5) eland,
(6) redbilled oxpecker on buffalo, (7) white rhinoceros, (8) leopard,
(9) African elephant, (10) kudu.

# MPUMALANGA

*The rugged and unpredictable paradise of Mpumalanga comprises undulating grasslands of the Highveld descending to the rocky bushveld sliced by river valleys and punctuated with occasional shrub on a distant horizon that separates searing sands from a brilliant blue sky. This is the Africa of textbooks, a world of flaming sunsets, haunting bird calls and herds of wild antelope.*

The Mpumalanga heartland is a world quite different to any other in Africa. Untamed wilderness areas teeming with wildlife of every description are interspersed with charming little gold-rush towns, tiny hamlets geared almost entirely to local farming communities, and small but impressive private game reserves – all of which, in turn, are serviced by bustling urban centres such as Witbank, Middelburg and Nelspruit.

In parts as dry as a bone and, in others, awash with the occasionally torrential waters of the region's rivers and streams, winter and early summer sees banks of mist descend on an otherwise rather parched landscape. This extraordinary land is the heart of conservation country, a priceless stretch of protected grassland and bushveld.

There is indeed a wealth of game parks and nature reserves in the southern subcontinent, and it is thus a haven for every type of conservationist and naturalist, but nowhere is this more apparent than in that jewel of Africa's conservation crown – the Kruger National Park, and the luxurious private game reserves that skirt its western border. Kruger is justifiably renowned for some of the most spectacular wildlife scenery on the continent. The sensitive ecology of the area depends on a perfect balance within its fragile ecosystems – from riverine forest to acacia-dotted savanna – and thus was born a number of tireless conservation efforts to preserve the natural environment of the region. At the same time, however, remarkable attempts have been made here to accommodate the all-important tourism market that has contributed quite considerably to the coffers of the broader region.

Be it the dry grasslands, the intermittent waters that have their source in the Great Escarpment or the rich indigenous vegetation, the natural resources are a vital source of life for the animals and plants that inhabit this veld and allow for a remarkable display of the capabilities of both the flora and fauna that make their home here in this wonderland of nature.

RIGHT *The Mpumalanga horizon is broken only by the silhouette of an occasional baobab, indigenous resident of the region for thousands of years.*

LEFT  *A country that boasts a number of records in the animal kingdom, South Africa is home not only to the world's largest land mammals – the elephant, white rhino and hippopotamus, respectively – but also the fastest (the cheetah), the smallest (the pygmy shrew) and the tallest, the giraffe (left), the most conspicuous inhabitant of the Mpumalanga thornveld.*

BELOW  *Much of the bushveld habitat of the country's northern stretch is, in the most part, a relatively dry region during the winter months when rains are virtually non-existent. As a result, its seasonal rivers and dams, such as the Kanniedood, are the lifeblood of the wildlife population.*

RIGHT *King among the beasts of the Mpumalanga bushveld is the lion, the largest of Africa's big cats. Its tawny coat provides excellent camouflage against the buff-coloured grasses of its arid environment, but it is usually under cover of darkness that the hunters of the pride – most often the females – draw on their fearsome combination of sheer strength and mass, powerful muscles and razor-edged teeth to take down their prey. The range of diet of this carnivore extends from giraffe to the small, but potentially lethal porcupine – its sharp quills embedded in the jaw of a lion can lead to infection and eventually kill even a male adult, which may weigh as much as 200 kilograms (440 pounds).*

OPPOSITE *The series of exclusive private retreats clustered around Dullstroom, a tributary stream of the Crocodile River, offer fine fly-fishing facilities on the area's trout waters. Brown trout were introduced to the inland waters in the lower reaches of the KwaZulu-Natal Escarpment in the late nineteenth century and were later distributed to freshwater streams and dams throughout the country. The rainbow trout, characterised by the purple-coloured stripe along its side, for which the area is best known today were released here in 1897.*

ABOVE AND RIGHT *A far cry from the wild places and wild game of the Kruger National Park and its adjoining private reserves are the trout-filled streams and dams around Dullstroom and the land to the west of Kruger. This is a world of tree-covered gorges, crystal waters and luxury hideaways such as Critchley Hackle Lodge (above) and the Rattray Reserve at Mount Anderson (right), catering almost exclusively to the fly-fishermen and other anglers who flock here during the height of the fishing season between March and September.*

LEFT  *Although vast tracts of the Mpumalanga bushveld are characterised by dry, sparsely vegetated plains, its rocky precipices are punctuated with striking waterfalls that make up the Waterfall Route. Among the most most impressive are the Lone Creek Falls, a tributary of the Sabie River, which cascades down a 68-metre (223 feet) rockface.*

TOP  *Surrounded by a small grove of wild peach, water berry and indigenous yellowwood trees is the 70-metre (230 feet) Bridal Veil Falls, one of the most captivating on the Waterfall Route.*

ABOVE  *The Lisbon Falls, just north of Graskop, comprises some three separate waterfalls tumbling from the collection of pools at the top of the 95-metre (312 feet) cliff.*

OPPOSITE  *Although in the dry season the Berlin Falls are little more than a steady trickle escaping from a narrow spout in the rock wall, the summer rains turn it into a torrent that falls some 80 metres (262 feet).*

ABOVE   *The jacaranda-studded terrain of the Barberton district offers a fascinating diversion of outdoor adventure from the more urban attractions of the historic gold-rush town.*

ABOVE *The subtropical splendour of Huala Lakeside Lodge near White River is virtually surrounded by the waters of a large dam, allowing all the rooms and suites of this upmarket lodge uninterrupted views.*

TOP  *Named in honour of a prospector who sought his fortune in the gold yielded by this stony ground, the Bourke's Luck Potholes were carved by the abrasive action of the Blyde River.*

ABOVE CENTRE  *The Three Rondavels range takes its name from the trio of distinctly hut-like peaks that skirt the Blyde River Canyon Reserve.*

ABOVE AND RIGHT  *The Blyde River Canyon is a breathtaking series of towering buttresses and forrested inclines that forms the centrepoint of the 27 000-hectare (66 700 acres) national reserve of the same name.*

ABOVE *The sweeping view of the Mpumalanga Lowveld is punctuated in the far northwest by the Ohrigstad Dam, one of a series of catchment bowls – both natural and man-made – that service the densely cultivated farmland of the region.*

LEFT *Worth far more than the fortune in gold said to be hidden in the area by Paul Kruger, president of the Boer republic, when he fled into exile in 1990, the district of Barberton is a treasure-house of the natural heritage of the Lowveld.*

OPPOSITE LEFT *One of the most spectacular viewpoints from the equally breathtaking Blyde River Canyon is God's Window, an untamed wilderness of lush rainforest.*

OPPOSITE RIGHT *Located in the heart of the Mpumalanga thornscrub, the tiny settlement of White River, with its charming country club and small but flourishing arts-and-crafts industry, provides a quiet retreat from which to explore the Mpumalanga Lowveld.*

OVERLEAF *Looking out over the edge of the ancient Escarpment, the little town of Graskop – itself not yet 100 years old – offers the most generous panorama of all the views across the ageless of the Mpumalanga Lowveld.*

## PHOTOGRAPHIC CREDITS
*(CPL = Cape Photo Library)*